THE NORTHERN STRANGER

LYSANDER KEMP

THE NORTHERN STRANGER

RANDOM HOUSE · NEW YORK

FIRST PRINTING

To LYLE and AMY GLAZIER

ACKNOWLEDGMENTS

All but one of these poems were written during Army service in Panama, Ecuador, and Puerto Rico, 1942-1945. Certain of them have appeared in *Poetry: A Magazine of Verse*, *The Kenyon Review*, and *Foreground*. Grateful acknowledgment is made for permission to reprint them here.

The poems in this book were submitted in partial fulfillment of the degree of Master of Arts in the Boston University Graduate School.

CONTENTS

Good Neighbor

GOOD NEIGHBOR

Now who will seek and winningly befriend
such arrogance out of the jungle?
Open the taut lips and the tribal mind?
Who will unbend and how will he unbend
to neighborly ways the body that slides in shadow
lightly like a column of mist or a ghost,
but fronts the northern stranger stiff as a post?

And who will seek and somehow coax from sleep
the destitute in the alley?
He sags in a doorway under a giant hat
with knees on chest and head on knees in a heap.
Who from our easier cities will come to his crumbling
tragic city and stand him straight and strong,
from love and goodness of heart, for nothing, a song?

—THE NORTHERN STRANGER

FASHIONS OF *LA LIBERTAD*

In the dirt road of the dirty town, the little
Ecuadorian soldiers march without shoes,
untidy and sad but oh perfectly at home
amongst the dogs and goats and potbellied children.
Everyone, it seems, walks barefoot in that town,
the *peón*, the crone, the cripple, the mother, all
shamelessly barefoot; all but the tall American
soldier striding in glittering shoes, who says,
"These people are no good."

But what they possess,
he is without. He walks in shoes, but they walk
shod in despair, unpolished but everlasting.
His uniform is handsome but they wear poverty,
not trim like khaki but durable to death.
He smiles now and soon he will scowl or laugh,
but their faces are not twisted, are beautifully calm
with *dolór, dolór,* the dark grief of the Indian.

ADMONITION

Plume of flesh, *pluma de carne*, shaken
in the night, in the day's light, in today's weather,
happy to stride, to sing, I am mistaken
to forget with all my heart that I am a feather
of blood and skin on a flimsy quill of bones.
I stride among cripples, blind to a brother shape
wrenched into accusation, deaf to the moans
of importuning, the machete-word of hate.
I sing among beggars, *chiu chiu* in slums
like untended graveyards, *chiu chiu* to dead
faces blankly peeping from crooked tombs,
to Pablo, asleep in the street, who has no bed.

Pluma de carne, feather of flesh among feathers,
sing but remember, stride but remember your brothers.

THE SPEECH OF THE GENERAL

People of this land, the starving, the dog-tired,
you that are poor, impoverished, penniless, come—
I give you seven acres of fertile nothing,
seven to every family, my pitiful people,
because I love you.

Come my ulcerous festering cancered leprous
consumptive paralyzed club-footed syphilitic
people—I give you a warm bowl of nothing,
three times every day and free for the asking,
because I love you.

Soldiers and beggars, farmers and workers and cripples,
clerks and laborers, pimps and peddlers and poets,
come along now and vote, I give you the splendid
chance to say nothing to your hearts' complete content,
because I love you.

Come to a new communion—your holy blood
shall be changed to gold, the blessed sweat of your limbs
to a simple hacienda. You know I am humble,
detesting speeches. I cry to you now only
because I love you.

SCENERY FOR A NICE LADY

Out of Gurabo, northward up from the plaza,
San Justo Road goes up and over the hills,
beautiful all the way—views of the valley,
the ploughed patches, the lavender-blooming cane,
the river sweetly repeating its easy turns.
Beyond the gap is the grand view to San Juan,
to the harbor, the haze of the sea, and the blue sea.

But there in San Juan is the frightful swarming section
of stilted rickety shacks constructed of rubbish
above polluted water and stinking flats.
Its name is not The Mud, it is *El Fanguito*—
The Little Mud. . . . When I first heard it, I winced
at the tragic laugh in the diminutive of affection.
Never go in, you will not come out of it happy.
Never come here, never go down to New York,
keep to your neat house if you want to keep happy.
All views are spoiled at the end by something awful,
by the little children wading in sewage water.

Too bad—but even in Paradise, I am told,
the faucet running milk and honey leaks,
drip drip drip all night, and they call the plumber,
but he never rouses out of his golden bed.

ON A WALL IN PUERTO RICO

For Narciso Dobal

Here is a chemist's work, garish and rude,
painted with pure colors and unmixed anguish.
A heavy tragic figure slumps on a shattered
column, the man is twisting, face in hands;
a woman sags in the door of a mountain shack,
looking out at nothing—the line of the leaning
arms is simple despair, or it is defiant,
as if to break the frame down and break free.
Under the painting are five Disasters of War.
Together a little chemist and Goya speak,
superbly or not but the voice is nothing, the words
and why the words are spoken, this is all.
They speak of war's disasters, disasters of peace,
indelicate talk, and we can take heart: the breath
fails in a throat but another man stands up
and speaks, crudely or neatly, as he is able.
If the words are ever lost, if nobody says them,
that is the end. That is good night, and the night.

A POST CARD FOR RUTH

If the derisive music sweetens
and the fierce eyes turn to buttons,
if the outrageous mocking snigger
chokes to apologetic giggles,
and the sharp lines go fuzzy, and anger
simpers, and protest snaps its fingers—
drop me a line, and we shall meet to carve
our headstones chip and chop, and dig our graves.

THE FAULTY HAG

El Fanguito, Puerto Rico

Passing the slums, the tragedies in doorways,
he glanced at his nails or nothing and praised the sun.
No pity, dismay, not even disgust: his look
was calm as a cow's. Why, damn him, why?
The motion pictures taught him the torn enchantment
is patched as good as new; he learned in the comics
the hearts of the poor are made of gold and fun.
Why was he not piteous, why not astounded?
Because the scene was dirty and too dreary,
with no imaginable happy ending, or not
American through and through nor in technicolor?
He thought that *El Fanguito* was not real?
True, in the picture that hag limping through mud
with a mad stare would croon, or bake a cake . . .
or might at least look up, and smile for the soldiers.

LANDSCAPE

The mist concealing the hills is gray and steady,
soft to the look but the look cannot enter;
the hand can enter but touches nothing. The mist
is mist—I say it in plain English, the white man's
language—here in the valley in the damp morning.

Plain and true . . . but the smoke is true also.
The smoke of this landscape fumes from the long burning
of shoes Rosita never owned, of the sweat
as hot as tears of Carlos Quiñones ploughing
his perpendicular slope. It fumes from the deep
guitar of Juan del Valle, the smoke of grief
with the song of grief more like a wail than a song,
hopelessly rising there in the tragic hills.

The sun will dissolve the mist, but sun will not clear
this air (Oh what will ever clear this air?)
of despair, the pitiful smoke, the bitter burning.

FANTASTIC CONVERSATION

—Who is it walking behind me?

                              —No one, Señor . . .
the night mist in the figure of a drunkard.
—Who is it speaking? I hear somebody speaking.
—Nobody, Señor, nobody . . . only a trace
of shadow in the figure of a nobody,
or else a nobody in the figure of a shadow,
traipsing you down the road. Why do you tremble?
I am nothing. I am the mountain wind.
The bamboo creaks like a stair in a haunted house,
but trees are not assassins. Easy, Señor.
—I tremble at night. In sunlight the various slopes
delight me like Vermont, but the dark upsets me.
I was a brave boy in the dark. I never
shied on the road in the robber-hiding wood
or screamed at hobgoblins cackling in my closet;
now I walk quickly and talk to nothing. And lately
I dreamed I strolled at dawn by a tiled canal
and a peg-legged whiskery seafaring idiot fellow
put out to sea in a crazy peach-basket boat,
hoisting a painted sail, bearing up-current,
chanting obscenely to a trim ballet of dolphins.
A shabby girl said, "He is our one salvation."
—A bad dream, Señor. Why did she say that?
—God knows. And I dream of a mad old man dying
in a dark room. At first he grins like a wolf,

but the grin loosens and fails and the eyes lid,
the body assuming the secrecy of defunction;
then out of the body, floating up and shaking
in the dim air in a rapid trilling of birdsong
and oboe music, a miniature of the body
shines a firefly green, blessedly smiling;
and drifts through the pane and streams off to the moon
like a green comet, announcing a new cadaver.
The shabby girl says, "He was our one salvation."
—A bad dream, Señor.

                    —Something is wrong . . .
myself or my world or the world and I together.
—I chop the cane with an old machete, Señor,
in the valley fields of a stranger, for too little money.
We live in a tin hut on the next hill up,
my wife, my seven children, my coughing father.
Something is wrong, American.

                    —Something is wrong
with your world and mine and the whole world.
I envied the free savage once, perceiving
none but honest animal wrongs; but then,
in a certain wind on the Isthmus, I lay awake
hearing a drum in the jungle under the hill,
a slack dreary thudding . . . it was the savage,
unable to comprehend and afraid to accept
the Northern ways and magic, calling without hope
to his own desolate uncomprehending people.
Something wrong.

　　　　　　　　—Where could I go, American?
Where is it good?
　　　　　　　　—Something is wrong in my country.
If the white bones and red flesh wear a black
skin . . .
　　　　　　　—My boy is a soldier. The Colonel says
my boy is black, my brother's boy is white.
They are both good sons. What is black and white,
American?
　　　　　　　—Nothing: tell your boy it is wrong,
but tell him to hold his tongue and take it standing;
he can do nothing, but tell him he will have friends.
Too, if the mathematician drinks, if the grocer
suggests a liberal doubt . . . wrongs in my country,
here, and the few countries I know. Felipe,
Carlos—what is your name?—I thought it was good
here on this island: Cabiya said it was good.
We flew across water in misted morning light
and down a swampy coast to Curaçao;
then over the city, and slanting off to the north,
over the crinkling whitecap-speckled sea
at such a height we shivered and clapped our hands;
then finally over the patterns in green and beige,
and the hills in russet and green, of Puerto Rico,
and columns of cloud standing up on your land.
—But something is wrong, Señor. What can we do?
—Pray for a dragon to shamble out of the sea
and gobble the wicked. Pray for a unicorn

[23]

to stab its magical purifying spike
in the dirty fount of the minds of the world's people.
Luis, Miguel . . . *amigo* . . . I think we can only
try and hope. And maybe we can do nothing,
nothing at all, nothing whatever, nothing
for trying, nothing but nothing: I sometimes think so.
—I know the word "nothing," Señor. Is that all?
—Maybe. Maybe a little . . . little by little.
—*Poco a poco.* I say in the field, "Nothing."
I say in the night, with too much rum, "A little."
But now I see the lights of Gurabo. Shadows
live on the hill, Señor. I must go home.
—Maybe nothing . . . but maybe a little. Good night.
—*Buenos noches, hermano.*

                              —Good night, brother.

LA CADENA VERDE

A Painting by José Torres Martinó, P.R.

He stands with his back against the standing cane,
right hand clutching a green chain and left hand
poised at his shoulder clutching the trim machete.
This is the final instant of his decision,
but all the story is here; the young cane-cutter
now perceiving the green links of necessity
lying across his feet like an anaconda.
That snaky chain will squeeze his life out early
(sugar is white . . . how can it not be red?),
and the cane-knife is up. But there is no ending now,
this year or next. The man will strike, or not,
but whether to cut the chain is whether to die
in rural or city destitution, is whether
to run from country anguish to grief in the gutters.
Oh it is horribly vain, it is equally futile,
whether he cuts, or sprawls in the hot field weeping.

—IN MY TIME

IN OUR TIME

Violent codger superbly ranting,
proud of his passions, old Yeats implored
a crazier hatred, caught the cry,
"Send us war in our time, O Lord!"
—cried it makes whole and hale a wanting
mind and it skins a cataracted eye.

Here is a wicked great old man,
we said, and clucked, and loudly praised
that what he said he thought was true.
Yeats was on the side of the crazed,
of the fool surely and Crazy Jane
and somewhat of him most fierce and his Nazi crew.

And Chamberlain, mildewed, waving proper
symbol-umbrellas or walking-sticks:
"A bumbler," we said, "but give him time."
And he dickered smoothly with lunatics,
he fed all Europe into the chopper.
"Peace in our time," he lisped as smooth as slime.

ECLOGUE

After the music was tried and shot, the vow
hanged by the neck, the skeleton starved, the shawl
of the mother clubbed in the yard . . . there is peace now.

In the ruined hour of the destroyed afternoon,
the year of the bombing, Peace from a splintered wall
of the blasted city tootles her sweet tune.

The sweet child at her feet is laughing. He plays
with his toys—a twisted joy, his toes, a doll,
a bullet, and all his broken coming days.

WORDS FOR THE FUNERAL OF MUSSOLINI

Sir, we blush, Sir, we convulse with shame,
that you hang here by the feet like a dead hog.
We hurried, forgive us, that was unseemly, forgetting
to string you up correctly, Sir, by the neck.
But nothing can spoil your finest hour, your people
about you, showing their love and tongues, showering
your corpse with flowers of spittle, saluting with boots.
And here is the coffin lined with shavings, perfect
for one so grand who died without ostentation.
Sir, the people are waiting, farewell, but first
permit me to place on your bare breathless chest
a wreath. I fear it is ugly (you killed the flowers,
but not without cause, we know, and a fair trial),
but here is the wreath (such as it is), of cabbage
and wigs and dead toads, and bandages intertwining,
and R. I. P. spelled out with snouts of jackals.
(I fear it smells.) Farewell.
Take him away.

THE DISSEMBLER

Subtle destruction wholly delights her mind:
with girl-bright eyes she riddles how to destroy
her slacking lover with glances sweet and kind,
with sleeking hands, a mimicry of joy
and love, so neatly done but oh untrue!

—If I were a bombardier crouched above Munich
remembering Grandsire remembering German brew
and German tunes and blossoms, I might be sick . . .
then subtle aim, cry "Jesus!" cry "Bombs away!"—

But in the act she knows her plot too savage,
and gives it over in tears and true dismay,
in truest love: she has the choice, being free.
So Love and War, though one in an old adage,
have at the worst this dear disparity.

TRANSPORT TO ECUADOR

Leaving Balboa, the little gulls and the filthy water,
passing green hill-islands, passed into the slick Pacific.

Once I should have cried denial
that I could voyage off in no ecstasy,
with no more thought and joy than when I rode
the poky train from Boston to Canton Junction.

But we ignored the blue bulging,
the dolphins arching over and curving under,
the fish that skim like a boy's glider:
for we must discover the drinking-fountain
and ask a sailor How is the food? Rotten? and learn
to walk like sailors the out-of-kiltering deck.

We ignored the Galapagos
(incredibly barren, the waste brown islands);
for Hugo, he vilified New England.
And we had crossed the Equator without knowing it.

At night we bedded on the cool deck
rolled into our blankets and feet bumping heads,
and talked of home a little, and slept tight:
scarcely glancing into the sky
at the tropic stars enormous and legendary
over the sea's rolling sibilant intricate surface.

[33]

REVEILLE HERE AND NOW

The palm by the door cleanly green because near,
the palms across the drill-field smoky blue,
and only the peaks of the tall hills up clear,
the flanks and foothills hid by a wall of haze—
that is the way a day begins, all new
and clearing to green, here in our valley days.
I stand at attention waiting to answer *Here!*
but my glance goes to the palms, the soft bamboos
enhancing the river, the mighty feather curled
around The Anvil; sweetly these appear.
There is no looking ahead, I must not lose
a morning look at this green surrounded world,
a palm hiding no sniper, hills where the sound
of thunder brings rain, not the heart's blood, to the ground.

SIMPLE SLUMBER

The car's flaring light
creates a moving microcosm, a world
we approach always but cannot enter, whirled
in the black of country night.

The mongrel poised in the grass,
now blind as a stone and changed to stone by fright,
has precious stones for eyes; to left and right
the trees loom and pass,

the double dazzles race
from the dark, the twin procession streams alas
like specters out of the black wall or morass
or gulf of outer space.

But we are moved to no dread,
no wonder. They pass, and vanish without trace.
This real but racing world is too vivid to face,
too bright for a tired head. . . .

For where we are going is where
in immobile barracks the stationary bed
is a void of simple slumber. The half dead
can lie steady and empty there.

We look, as if counting sheep,
at the flashing marvels, the cur's diamantine stare,
the stream of phantom trees. We are bored to despair.
We want the nothing of sleep.

WISHING POEM

The bells of Guayama ring the quarter hour
all day and half the night, or all perhaps—
they rang, and a shutter banged in a cool wind,
and perhaps they tolled for me, but I was sleeping.
I woke to the bells and the sun up clear and a boy
proclaiming oranges under my plaza window.
My sleep was spoiled, but the boy's cry was sweet
as the sweet fruit he cried, compared to the brash
brazen get-up-in-the-morning bugle. I rose,
washed and ate, and sat on a plaza bench
under the huge symmetrical trees, admiring
the sun, the *señoritas*, the gleaming church—
its door is Corinthian, I think the towers are French,
but the church is Spanish and right and fine to admire,
and the bells all morning rang the quarter hour.

So what? So what have I said, so what am I saying?
The lines come without labor, saying nothing,
saying a peddler woke me, I loafed in the plaza,
Guayama is nice in the sun. Behind or under,
unsaid in the slack lines and remembered languor,
there is a fierce wish. I wish for peace
more than I wished for anything before,
more than I guessed that I could wish for anything.
Almost, I pray for peace. I am a soldier
who has fired only at paper, and bled only

when shaving with salt water. Yet I can wish
peace for men who fight for peace and hardly
recall it, peace for children who have not known it,
peace on earth; I wish it so, it half
seems wrong to want so calm a thing so fiercely.
No, wishing takes no towns—but the wish now
can afterwards be love. Now wish for peace,
and when it is ours at last, it must be loved.
We know how it is taken while we sleep;
the haggard boy could tell us, if he had time,
how dirty sleeplessly hard it is to recover.
Love it for keeps. Guard and love. Be a lover.

AFTER

Snow, and the train is late. The grinning doctor
smoothens his famous pewter-colored smooth hair.
The tidal wave ascends. A door is shut.
In Dedham a dead dog putrefies the air.

Why can I see presentiments of dismay,
omens of rage and destruction? Now we have paid
in tears or years or very life for peace.
It is ours now, but I am still afraid—

for there was a bullet made and meant for me
and bullets for you and the grocery boy and John
and plenty of bullets for old Aunt Grace and all
and a small bullet for the small dog asleep on the lawn.

We paid for peace, but it is too easily broken.
I will keep all my portents safe and sound,
always in mind, and not yet forget the warning
snow in the air, the dog dead on the ground.

—A HEADFUL OF SCENES

GUAYAQUIL, 1943

The scraggly fields, and cattle staunch on the tracks,
lolligag children hawking beer and papaya,
the bone-bag curs, the vulture-gargoyled shacks—
it was a drear approach. But the city was fabled;
imagining quaint splendors, I crossed the Guayas.

By streetlight, the florid porticoes and fronts,
where toughs and *putas* lurked, were standing rubble;
I dodged convulsive drunks in bamboo slums.
By daylight, then—but every street was the haunt
of sleek dudes and tender diligent pimps,
the grandiose façades were defiled and acrumble,
I strode among beggars who flaunt their shocking limbs.

In Rocafuerte Park I drooped to a bench,
darkly and peevishly rhyming wench and stench.

MEMENTO OF GUAYAQUIL, 1945

It is a queer city, in a queer country. Nothing
is middling, as in New England. Buildings are stone,
flowery and huge, or else of split bamboo.
Where lawny suburbs ought to be, it is slums.

From the huge door of the stone hotel, a blond
American soldier in plain sight for gawking,
but gawking back, I watched the man of business,
the dude, the lady, pass in their fine clothing,
the *peón* in pants and sweat. I heard the click
of better people pattering by in their shoes,
and under, the barefoot primitive soft padding,
jungle feet on cobbles, the ocelot step.
Nothing was halfway, nothing I found was middling,
as in New England; it was all weeds or all clover.

And thinking, "Here some are so well to do, and the poor
pitiable poor so poor," and thinking, "Here
I am halfway in between and glad to walk
in the middle (born and brought up to walk just there),"
I joined to Guayaquil staring up or down,
to Guayaquil pattering or lightly padding by,
my middling look, my weedy foot and clover.

FIRST VIEW

Here is Gurabo, dirty-pale in the sun,
here is the beggar, the pimp, the cripple; and look,
here comes mad Ramón, lashing his cane
at the bony mongrel doting in his wake.

But there is the road out up to high ground,
rising and looping in and out of the line
of broken slopes, the hills always unowned
except by the lonely, never by us, by Spain.

There you can look away off and breathe clean
and speak as clear as water and stand up tall;
there in the tilting patterns of earth and green
a man can shut his mouth, and sit still.

SAN JUAN

A *Décima*

Here are Spanish seas,
Felipe said, and was King,
and the vast escarpments ring
the city. *Maria y Luis*
in a lopsided heart, these
are not the King's endeavor.
But walls he ordered never
to fall, they chip, and fall
to time; the bashful scrawl,
it is for ever and ever.

A HEADFUL OF SCENES

There was Culebra to port, Vieques to starboard,
and dead ahead, St. Thomas tall in the haze.
I rode the bow in sun, from Puerto Rico
between two islands, dreaming to write a poem
of scapes and glimpses in full color, ending
again on an old theme. And yes indeed,
I saw the vermillion roofs and storybook buildings
up and down the hillside, all as promised,
the Danish fort, the flamboyant trees, the black
lank-legged girls. But this was not enough;
two days can never blossom into a poem
unless they root in every living day . . .
my eyes were entranced, but it was only looking.
I rode the bow back with a headful of scenes
and a heavy heart from knowing I was blind.
And there was Vieques to port, Culebra to starboard,
and Puerto Rico dead ahead in the sun.

GUARACHA

Bewildered by strange music, the shake
of dark dancers in a strange rhythm,
the dark boy singing his passion out,
Yo *te quiero* from the big throat
immediately, beyond mistake—

bewildered, uneasy, scratching a thumb,
I saw your sungold hair and tall
beauty and straighter Northern grace
on the wagon-road under the mountain,
on the wide porch, in the daisy-field—
but not here, not twisting in this place;
and suddenly I was sick for home.

REMEMBERING CAPE COD

For Miss Park

Here on a crest in Panama, the body
is cooped in walls of green, of locking leaves
that flourish and die together the full year.
Mind flies out; it sees and hears to northward
a rapid leaning wave collapse and spill
to a crumple, a soft roil of rubble and bubbles
and sandy brine ascending the sleek rise—
water music at ebb or flood, the dear
andante dearer than Mozart, than any sound
except of voices constantly remembered . . .
the music sinks to a rustle, and mind returning
stares from body's eyes at bough and bird,
at body's home.
                    Considers the poky sloth:
He dangles topsy-turvy out on a branch
of this forever Spring, in coat of buff
and all day chumbling into his umber face.
He never sees from his green lookout the flowing
margin of night engulf the Persian slopes
and the peaks go under like islands going under;
chumbles by day, slumbers by night, nor chills
nor thrills to vision time a flooding tide
careening perpetually to no turn or ebb;

famous weakwit, exists like any beast
in the simple present of no despair nor rapture.

Considers wryly those who could envy sloths!—
the frightened of man, of John and Jean and Juan,
who cry from turrets against the love of man
(the trap, one says, that snapped on Christ), who cry,
"Beware the Bandarlog, the flock, Chicago,
live like the stoic eagle!" . . . sloths are stoic,
no Mardi Gras in their arboreal haunts;
and the frightened of time who dream the dreamless land
or clockless demesnes of dream beyond the glass,
who mourn for morals and blooms and Greeks . . . the sloth,
requiring time for sleeping, time for feeding,
has time enough, and that is that is that.

But those who laugh at such and brag they grapple
the reins from Marvell's charioteer and drive
at their own pace and pleasure, they live no happier,
sink in no easier final waters of peace:
the badgered Serb still laughs at Diocletian,
who hid his animal ears and killed his barbers
but was undone by a somewhat slyer jack;
and crazy Lear, rampaging the terrible heath
in a pother of clacking boughs and cracking skies,
he doomed to lightning-bolts the unbending oak,
power imploring power to shatter power—
but Humphrey tittered, and went to bed at noon.

Pity the strong. He is so set about,
so pestered and importuned, how can he sleep?

Considers also, the homesick mind considers
the fidgeting marmosets, the armadillo,
lizards and birds in the morning in the green shadows.
But always too soon the mind gives up, the creatures
fading into the jungle, the jungle fading:
and always a reach of lion-colored dunes
arising blots all Panama from mind,
whelms and is the scene, and a wave spills
and gathers, leans, and spills, and mind knows only
a northward scape and hears a sound of water,
this land annihilated by distant music,
by the dear andante dearer than any sound
except of voices constantly remembered.

A FEW NOSTALGIC LINES

Here I can see in a green circle the rough
or feminine shapes of the hills around Caguas,
remember the white swan-breasted Maine hills,
the Paris-green bonbon peaks of Panama,
yes, and picture, beyond the trough of Stone City,
the splendid running-away immobile sea-swell
of Iowa hills, with the spherical trees for bubbles.

But what I want for hills—my taste is plain
and homesick lately—are dunes, the little barren
dunes of Cape Cod even the toad can climb.

HOW TO GO HOME

To know your native place and proper home
(the house on the dunes above the glittering bay),
its tug on your heart, its full felicity, roam
(but remember her sea-streaming, leaning and laughing
as she ran up the tilt of the tawny shore);
and then go back easily, go back simply,
as though you had only walked to the corner store.

—THE CARIBOU AND THE COBBLER

BOY GOING AWAY

A Drawing by DIEGO RIVERA

The boy will ride away, but he tarries still
in the swept yard on his little trim-footed horse.
There is the road to the village and over the hill
to some place, different living better or worse,
but he tarries, murmuring good-bye to his bent mother
looking up to his face that is tenderly hard
(he is almost a man), and good-bye to his envious brother,
to the leaping dog, and staring at hut and yard
and all as if for the first time or the last.
He is a Mexican boy—but that pain and pride
whelmed up in a Swedish or any boy at the mast
as the hills dimmed and dropped. Not one can hide,
however perfectly steady his voice and eye,
the glory of going, the agony of good-bye.

THE SEMBLANCE OF DEFUNCT

The slain importunate Denmark, stalking the height,
dropping dimly at cockcrow into Hell,
was Quince compared to my living haunt of daylight:
it seems there is no imaginable flesh
between the tight skin and the white skull!
A skeleton thinly bagged, the head being death's!

But he is so spry and affable, why can he so
enslit my eyes and sibilate my breath,
however made in the semblance of defunct?
And why can my steady mind so fashion absurd
light-of-day spooks, a friend . . .
                              I know, I know:
Here is the quick affrighting the quick with death.
Too scantly different, too visibly conjunct,
here is body alive or disinterred.

LAST VISION

Whom once in cloudy dreams he loved,
in a clear dream she set above
her umber locks a lightning-rod
(like bowsprit over figurehead)
to catch and ground what she most fears—
the perilous chain-lightning of ideas.

SMALL TALK

"He loves me, but dreads a life-sentence to jail,
bellowing like the Minotaur," she said,
"amazed, shouldering the stone perplexity
in which true loves are pent; but he shall fail
to break from our private prison till one is dead."
I loathed her classic mouthing of that decree,
her voice was liquid but bitter and too thin.
"Is not the truest love," I softly purred,
hoping my speech no more ridiculous,
"a walling out as well as a walling in—
two lovers within a summer garden, immured
to each from peddlers, checks, the supper bus;
and when they please, opening the gate together?"
Sweetly we deplored the deplorable weather.

THE LIE FROM THE JUNGLE

The days flamed; it seemed the perpetual green
writhed and was hostile; the vultures turned above,
diligent, ominous, patrolling their blue demesne.

True. But his distraught profession of love
was a profanation of friendship. It is a sweet
chatter that even the strictest lovers know,
neatly compounded of honor and fine deceit.
Friendship is honor wholly, or nothing.
                             So,
being the truest friends, the sudden lie
was palpable and coy, was self-confessed
before her rebuking paragraphs were dry.
And honor, so endangered, was redressed.

The dark monstrous vultures constantly sailed
their bright regions, but they had not prevailed.

OF BEAUTY TWICE

She fails us. They are false or dream
Who brag an intimacy thus,
For thus abstracted she is nothing,
And lips and locks are only foolish.
When I may waltz upon the whitecaps,
Then I shall make my overtures,
But skeptic still and of half hope.

It fails us. Though we trust it more,
An utter trust is folderol.
Here is a minor instance: tired,
I fetched a summer beach to mind,
But visioned only the white belly
Of a flung dogfish sun-corrupt,
Whereon the greenheads buzzed and fed.

PEDAGOGICAL

You daze your head with a bruit of horns and heralds,
reading the pomp, the campaigns, the Queen of Faerie,
totting the royal wivings and court quarrels;
or tread a blooming meadow, solitary
pupil to scrub-oak and philosopher cows;
or cluck with codgers the dry rot of fable.
The young, the young, quick and curious, how
are their minds to batten on silly kings and cattle?

We postulated once the constant teacher,
his ease preparatory, his lightest leisure.
I blame only the strictness of your pleasures.
Jaques, good sobersides, they are not wrong
to want your measures less than dancing measures:
they will not always be the immediate young.

SMALL BALLAD

The ghost ran in
the ghost whirled out
the ghost walked through shut doors clucking and whining
and flew about.

Señor Recuerdo sprang up from the sofa,
neat fellow now dressed in impeccable rage,
and reached for the rifle strung in webs, to kill
a ghost impertinent to middle age.

It was the ghost
of an old wrong
or shame or fiasco circling there like a stupid
detested song.

Señor Recuerdo fired, and handed
the gun back up to the spiders, and huddled in bed
stark naked in sorrow, suddenly knowing ghosts
are undying, the most living ghost is dead.

LITTLE PORTRAIT

In that room everything waits, waiting for noon,
the Lord, the mail, a total eclipse or a crime,
something or anything. There an old buffoon,
the banjo clock, secretly loses time,

waiting for yesterday. There the bloated divan
waits for Spring, and the rug waits for the step
of Dolores, the swarthy magic stranger, to liven
its tints, and heave its Persian blooms with sap.

Everything waits. The shadow waits on the floor
for night, and the lily waits for day in its pot.
And the room's tenant waits for a knock on the door,
that might be Life there knocking, and might not.

IN FIELD OR FLOOD

The wild creatures exist in the simple present,
a never-blasted Arcady. True, the foxhounds
gallop the trim talented fox to a kill,
but think! he is never hounded to thinking of death;
his foe is actual, children across the river
bolt up in bed to hear the clear pursuit.
And Rilke, circling a Duino garden, lamented
we turn too early or turn too late and never
of single mind like south-going birds; whirring
out of our muddle, we suddenly buck the wind,
and drop to freezing ponds. We know together
whale rollicking and whale stinking the breeze,
but in Ngong, among the beautiful hills,
the lion roams and roars—he is aware,
in his tawny magnificence, of no frailty.
I too was jealous, deluded by praise of cheetah
splendidly bounding, lizard utterly lizard.
I envied even the probity of snails!

But nonsense, all of this. *Tigrillo*, little
Peruvian tiger, the dappled ocelot,
is not aware his flesh is frail and doomed,
and I, who lack his jungle grace, foresee
defunction dead ahead (*O timor mortis!*).
Yet I can match his bliss of never knowing
with ecstasies of knowing beyond his wit,

and match his born superbities of body
with mental splendors passionately acquired—
his pretty pelt with a maybe insane Van Gogh,
his waiting crouch with the taut flawless tension
of a Yeats poem, his lissome limbs with Mozart;
and I can match his every last perfection.

No scorn, I was envious once; I shall not now
say "Brute creation!" out of the side of my mouth.
I shall praise all living against its opposite,
impartially praising the caribou and the cobbler,
the hill-fighter, the fox on the hill in the morning.

—YO SOY MEJICANO

TO THE VISIONARY

If ships once trim and trimly manned
lie fathoms under the whitecaps,
their captains lost and every hand,
then tell me, Captain, how shall we
with no sextant and no maps
raise land across a wicked sea
in a crude boat, or none perhaps;
clamber that lovely isle no lookout ever
sang from his perch in fine or fiendish weather?

LANDSCAPES BY LORCA AND DISNEY

There I saw in that fantastic landscape
the two rivers, one blood and the other tears,
and olive-trees heavily fruited with sobs,
and the guitar wailing of arrows without targets.

Elsewhere I saw in a confusion of landscapes
the lumbering precision of the cactus ballet,
a winged burro that smiled like an imbecile,
Baía in Hell's colors, the wicked witless bird.

But I was unable to weep, unable to laugh,
and have thus returned here where laughter
moves living flesh and sobs issue from lips.
Look, joy is right here. Heartbreak is near, listen.

SMALL VOICE FROM THE MUDDLE

Like a spent fugitive, babbling across the fields,
who hunts the cathedral to cry out, "Sanctuary!"
and startles the farmer's boy with a fierce question,
you startle me with pleading and fierce questions.
There is no hideout from what rides you down,
only the popular hideouts that are no good.
You ask, and I mention these; but surely you know.

The faraway isle is farthest away. *Frau* Koerwin
kissed her spouse, and Ritter his *frau*, and they sailed
to Galapagos, to a naked natural life.
(And ho! a tyrannical Baroness packed a pistol,
she was the world, and paradise was a shambles;
but there are millions of palmy remote islands.)
I know . . . your doctor tethers you in New England.

The church is nearer, it is an easier refuge,
its pews and blessings are right around the corner.
Ave Maria Santissima, the good Lord—
white and spotlessly white and faultlessly white—
is right around the corner, waiting for you.
Only to believe is important; without believing,
the depot, the bank, the poolroom are as safe.
I know . . . you cannot believe that you can believe.

There is no refuge half so near and dear
as the private world created in the head—
Arcady, Oz, or a still central sea
wherein you may disport like a lone dolphin.
I know of a crazy painter who capered in tropic
graveyards, dancing at night with a *fuego fatuo,*
the foolfire quivering over the not-embalmed;
and I saw the dickeybird peer from his silly world
of painted chips and snarls of light. That fellow
lives in the special perpetual bliss of the mad.
I know . . . you are of sound mind beyond hope.

So there they are, in my rough pentameters, all
impossible, vain, escape is vain, there is none.
The church, the private isle, the secret world
are walled or removed or hid in head but never
proof against life; any living is life.
But maybe there is a happier way to be happy.
As I see it (unless you choose defunction),
square in the midst is the one sanctuary.
The public world is personal there, the sky
is church; and Earth, however you may despair,
is the best and only blessed isle we know,
and always all yours all day all year and always.

FRAGMENTS OF AN IMPOSSIBLE POEM

Here is a Mexico, what I have put together
of a land I have never seen, from songs and pictures,
books and hearsay . . . an imaginary country
made of pieces ignorantly but fondly.

I hear the proud singer: "Yo soy mejicano . . .
I am Mexican, my land is wild," he sings.
"There is no land lovelier and braver than mine."

I think of Perejetes, the scabby saintly
idiot who painted stars on the floor of his hut
and angels on all the walls. He never said,
"I am going home." He said, "I am going to Heaven."
And he excommunicated the village priest.

"My land is wild," the singer cries, but a poet
said, "Suave patria . . . gentle fatherland . . .
the fatherland is impeccable and diamantine."

I stare at the mounted caballero, his gallop
set on country pottery, quaint and pretty.
(At home I saw the ladies and gentlemen ride
their costly horses, but none of them rode like this.)
The painted horse is crude, the head is too small—
but what a graceful neck, arching, swanlike!

The *caballero*, his pistols ready, is riding
to fight for the Revolution, for land and liberty.
Whether he gallops to fight for right or wrong,
who can say now, and whether to win a place
on or under that land? . . . but he is a dashing
caballero; surely the man will fight.

"*Nací despreciando la vida y la muerte,*" the singer
cries . . . "I was born contemptuous of life and death."
But the Indian huddled in darkness trembles and says,
"When the owl calls from the roof-tree, the Indian dies."

Oh this is impossible, this is absurd!—I know
for sure it is false, distorted, not the actual
honest-to-goodness country or anything like.
But how to know that country? If I go there,
learn the talk, the customs, the larger cities
and the smallest town in the most hidden province,
I know Mexico? I can never know that country,
never know any country to say I know it.
How do I know my own? My Massachusetts?—
a dozen towns, one city. Maine?—one city.
New Hampshire?—two towns. Vermont?—one town, one mountain.
Utah, Rhode Island, Georgia?—nothing nothing,
words in a book, words and lines on a map.
I think I can only want and try to know
my country, Mexico, any land on earth;
let nothing, no Northern blindness, no Western bias,

keep me from knowing more of anybody.
Yo *soy mejicano*—I am Turkish Peruvian Russian
Chinese Liberian, my skin is black white brown.
The planet Earth is my home. I like it here,
I have many neighbors. I look to know them better.